Dear San Antonio, I'm gone but not lost.

Bárbara Renaud González

Dear San Antonio, I'm gone but not lost.

LETTERS TO THE WORLD FROM YOUR VOTING RIGHTS
HERO WILLIE VELÁSQUEZ ON THE OCCASION OF HIS
REBIRTH

1944-1988-2018

BASED ON A TRUE STORY

by

Bárbara Renaud González

San Antonio, Texas

DEAR SAN ANTONIO, I'M GONE BUT NOT LOST.
LETTERS TO THE WORLD FROM YOUR VOTING RIGHTS HERO WILLIE VELÁSQUEZ
ON THE OCCASION OF HIS REBIRTH
1944-1988-2018

FIRST EDITION

Copyright © 2018 by Bárbara Renaud González

LIBRARY OF CONGRESS CONTROL NUMBER: 2018939903

RENAUD GONZÁLEZ, BÁRBARA

Dear San Antonio, I'm Gone but not Lost: Letters to the World from your Voting Rights Hero Willie Velásquez on the Occasion of his Rebirth 1944-1988-2018/Bárbara Renaud González. – Includes Map, Illustrations, photographs, bibliographical reference and index.

ISBN: 978-1-948955-01-0

Ordering Information:
Quantity sales: special discounts are available on quantity purchases by corporations, associations, and others. For details, contact the "Special Sales Department" at www.alazanstories.org.

Dear San Antonio, I'm Gone but Not Lost: Letters to the World from your Voting Rights Hero Willie Velásquez on the Occasion of his Rebirth. 1944-1988-2018 / Bárbara Renaud González. ISBN: 978-1-948955-01-0.

Select Illustrations: Feda Zidan, Patricia Cody

Dear San Antonio de Padua,
You are the patron saint of lost causes.
I am trying to find democracy.
Willie

DEAR SAN ANTONIO

CONTENTS

DEAR SAN ANTONIO

DEDICATION

To Mariana S. Ornelas, a beloved friend who worked for Willie and had faith that I would tell his story. Gracias.

To the Dudley T. Dougherty Foundation, who provided the early funds so that I could begin to shape a book worthy of Willie.

To the Velásquez family, Tex-Mex royalty.

To the future voters of Texas

and

to all who believe in democracy,

especially Joaquín Ávila,
RIP.

DEAR SAN ANTONIO

FOREWORD

Dear teachers,

Just like Willie, I was born and raised on the Westside of San Antonio. But I didn't know who he was until a few years ago. He is not generally taught in the schools.

I have fond memories of my parents' active involvement in community service. My parents voted regularly and kept up with local, state, and national politics. They participated in block-walking, and we put up signs in our front yard. My dad wrote letters to the newspaper editor, offering his opinions about critical issues of the day. He listened to radio shows and called in. He was very active in Communities Organized for Public Service (COPS). During the elections, my mom worked the polls at Ogden Elementary. It's possible that my parents mentioned Willie Velásquez, but I was a teenager when Willie was beginning his career, and somehow, the conversations between my parents did not stick with me.

By 2014, I had become the principal of Hillcrest, an elementary school in the San Antonio Independent School District (SAISD). Hillcrest is nestled on the southwest side of San Antonio and provides services to a demographic consisting of 98 percent Hispanic families. Hillcrest opened more than 100 years ago and many of our families have great-grandparents, grandparents and parents who attended school there. There is a keen sense of community and pride in the Hillcrest community. One day while enjoying a cup of coffee, my husband David shared a story he was reading in the morning newspaper about the upcoming Willie Velásquez Day, on May 9th. I also learned that a digital book had been written by Bárbara Renaud González and was available digitally on the Apple iPad. Because I grew up voting, I was inspired by

Willie's dogged determination to fight for our voting rights by registering millions of people to vote.

I also recognized a lovely young woman in the picture as the new community events coordinator for the BiblioTech library opening on the Southside. BiblioTech was slated to be the answer to my prayers for our community. It offers collections of downloadable e-books and audiobooks for all ages, including best sellers, classics, graphic novels, indie picks and so much more. It was important for our students and families to become aware of this goldmine that was going to be literally in their back yard. I wanted the coordinator to create awareness of this hidden gem in our community. Her name was Catarina "Cata" Velásquez.

When I did meet her, she was full of energy and excitement and so happy to share these valuable resources with our community. As is common in San Antonio, we ended up making a personal connection through *mi prima*, Esperanza Garza Danweber, a high school librarian. The two young educators had attended high school together. Cata never told me that her father was Willie. I seem to recall that *mi prima* revealed that detail to me later.

After I realized the connection, I became even more determined to share his story with my students. I asked my staff to make plans for a "Learning Week" to include various learning opportunities honoring Willie Velásquez. My staff and I created a two-week plan of events so that every classroom had an opportunity to watch the interactive book in our library (it was free). Our fifth-grade students, inspired by the book, created a play based on the interactive story for the fourth-graders and later presented it to the entire student body. We conducted a mock election. The students created wall-to-wall murals depicting Willie's neighborhood, his portrait, and his alma mater, St. Mary's University. The Pre-K students decorated their classrooms with American flags and marched in the parade chanting Willie's mantra, "Su voto es su voz!" Throughout the school, students decorated t-shirts and their faces with the lightning bolt image from the interactive book, all in honor of Willie.

Our school buzzed with excitement and energy. *The Boy Made of Lightning*, the first interactive children's book on the life of Willie Velásquez, gave them hope and the idea that their dreams and visions for their future were filled with possibilities. If a little boy from the Westside of San Antonio came to realize his dreams, perhaps they could, too.

We offered a voter registration drive and invited NALEO (The National Association of Latino Elected & Appointed Officials, a non-partisan membership organization) and the League of Women Voters. The students cast their vote for mayor. At the same time, I read about the writer who had written and produced *The Boy Made of Lightning*, Bárbara Renaud González. I messaged Bárbara, inviting her to present the story to my students during that week. I was honored and impressed that Bárbara responded immediately. We spoke on the phone for what seemed like hours. We have been *amigas* ever since.

I also contacted former city councilwoman Maria Antonietta Berriozabal as well as activist Rosie Castro, mother of former San Antonio Mayor Julián Castro and U.S. Congressman Joaquín Castro. And I reached out to the family of Willie Velásquez. I was determined to hear from *la gente* who had firsthand experience with and knowledge about our new hero, Willie Velásquez.

We were graced by the presence of the author. Ralph Velásquez, Willie's younger brother, and Debora Kuetzpal Vasquez, the artist/illustrator of the interactive book, also visited us.

While I've recently retired from Hillcrest to take care of my elderly mother, I volunteer in local, state and national elections. A shout out to my friends: Jane Velásquez, Rose Marie DeHoyos, Terry Mazuca Garcia, Frankie Gonzáles-Wolfe, Monica Ramirez Alacantara, Julie Torres, Irene Chavez y Juany Torres for staying engaged in the process. I am a certified deputy voter registrar and have recently been certified as an election judge. I wear my candidate buttons with pride! I am active in local, state, and national elections, and also serve as a county precinct chair.

I recently was invited to join the board of the Alazan Arts Letters & Stories (AALAS), where I am able to share ideas and *chisme* with Bárbara as she continues to research and write the untold stories of our (s)heroes.

During my tenure at Hillcrest, we commemorated Willie Velásquez Week every year. Every student deserves to learn about his (s)heroes. Trust me, there are many among us. To all the teachers and administrators, remember: ¡*Su voto es su voz*!

Terri Flores Lopez
Former Principal,
Hillcrest Elementary School
& Board Member of
Alazan Arts Letters and Stories (AALAS)

San Antonio, Texas
2018

INTRODUCTION

I got these letters from Willie

Let me say that I believe in ghosts, Santa Claus, and the devil with the rooster foot. Don't you? Lately, I've been hearing from Willie Velásquez, one of the most important and fiery people from Texas, specifically, San Antonio, a soulful city with rivers and creeks like a spider web of water.[1] A semi-tropical city with all kinds of palm trees, orange trees and Spanish wrapped-up with English, like the Christmas lights on the river at Thanksgiving. Heard of the Alamo? Yup, it's here, along with four other missions, a million people strong, and stories about war and borders, dancing on rooftops, the Polish and Germans, the French and the Jews and lots and lots of Mexicans fighting and some of them surrendering and others winning and

---

[1] Considered by many to be one of the most soulful and haunted cities in Texas – home to the Alamo and a vast network of creeks and rivers that served the dozens of indigenous communities that lived there. San Antonio was named for St. Anthony of Padua by the Spaniards. Founded in 1718.

1

it's been three hundred years since *San Anto*[2] was taken from the Native Americans who are still here. And we are celebrating that too and feeling guilty at the same time....

Willie grew up right here, on the Westside, *el Hueso*. The bone of San Antonio. We call it the barrio.

Lately, people have been getting these letters, and they bring them to me. I don't know why, only that Willie died 30 years ago this year, 2018. Something about he's stepping up, moving on, and now he's finding himself. Not lost anymore, no way. Has things he wants to get off his chest. Knows the way home to you now.

This is his story.

---

[2] "San Anto" is the colloquial version of San Antonio, a phrase used in the barrio.

Dear mamá,

This is Willie, your first-born. And your first-dead, too. Thirty years this May 9, 2018, can you believe it? The Big One told me I could write you now, that you are on your way to me, and that you'll get this letter for sure. That it's time for me to write everyone, because The One brought me here for a good reason, and The One says that letters don't lie...

You told me that it was 1944, World War II going on, and I was on my way to being born in Orlando, Florida, because papá was stationed there. First time you'd been outside of Texas. And when you got there, just a few months before I was born, marrying him even though your father didn't like him, didn't trust him, that woman showed up at the hotel room looking for him! Papá not wearing his wedding ring anymore.

But you made up, Mary Louise Cárdenas. No choice. You were barely 18 years old – William Cárdenas Velásquez, Sr., was 26. You were Catholic, and didn't, couldn't divorce. Not then. You were almost broke, far from home. And then I was born. May 9, 1944. On Mother's Day. Supposed to be this way. Me, William Cárdenas Velásquez, Jr.

Named for papá. And I became Billy – though later, it was Willie. Really like my name. Guillermo in Spanish. And you loved me very much.

I was the first of the five children you and papá had: Me. Stella. George. Ralph. David. But I was always your favorite, right? I was conceived in love, right? Cause the marriage sure didn't have much of that...

Mamá, you taught me so many things. When papá went off to Europe to serve in the war, you brought me home to San Antonio. You are the one who explained the world to me, taught me the rules, sang to me in Spanish, taught me how to read before I got into school. You taught me how to work hard. How to share. You taught me how to treat everyone the same. Papá taught me how to fish, not the same thing at all. I know I made you proud.

3

Most of all you taught me when you listened to my dreams. Smiled at me when I told you what I wanted to become, first thing in the morning and right before I went to sleep. The kind of man my father could never be. Yes, he worked hard at the plant, but he was never home. Why? You never answered, but I knew. I guess I was his replacement in a way. And in telling you my dreams, they began to come true. Mamá. You believed in me.

Dreams come true, mamá. Even if having those dreams meant that I was supposed to leave my family so soon, to come here way before you. My dreams came true because of you, mamá.

Con mucho amor pa' siempre,
Tu Willie

Dear mamá,

Remember when I saved that man after the flood? Remember? It was sunny like it always is after a thunderstorm. I decided to go exploring with Rudy, and you packed some tacos for the day, so I took a rope just in case we found something interesting. You told me, *mucho cuidado, mijito.*

And what a day we had! Left our *casita* on Laurel Street, walking all the way to Elmendorf. The creeks were flowing everywhere, it was like a buzzing, whooshing, rushing sound of water all around, and the water was talking to me, mamá. It said go this way, go that way – and Rudy and I did. We saw all kinds of dead dogs, *pansas infladas*, a million quacking ducks, messed up kites hanging on trees, one old shoe after another, broken chairs and tires and someone's recliner, can you believe it, floating everywhere.

Then we heard. Him.

The yelling. Desperate. *Ayúdenme!* Help me! A man's voice, over there! Rudy and I raced toward that voice, stumbling, tripping, getting cut and sliced with the brush and weeds, sticky and gooey with mud,

4

scratched by the tree limbs and sinking sometimes in the swampiness to our waists, but we found him in the middle of that sun-filled day, in the middle of nowhere, in the middle of so much roaring that no one heard but us. That man was trying to stay above the water but was bopping up and down. The rope!

The rope! *Ándale* Rudy!

Mamá, I threw it like the baseball champ I am, and didn't miss. And you always taught me to believe, not to get nervous about anything, and it worked! I didn't panic. Threw the rope and it spiraled in a perfect arc, like a missile, like a bomb for saving not destroying and once that man held on, we jumped in the creek and pulled him out.

I told you the whole story in the evening, and you were so proud of me. I was so mad, wanting to cry even though papá said men don't cry, but you understood. You told me that people were always dying in the floods in San Antonio.

You said it was a good thing for a man to have *sentimiento*. That I shouldn't listen to everything papá said. You told me to use *mi coraje*, which is really a passion for life (though some people just call it anger you said) and use it for something good. You said that's what it's for.

I remember the man's name, even though I don't remember all of it, I will know him when I see him again: Porfirio de la Luz Saenz. Been looking for him. *Como estás*, Porfirio? How did your life turn out? Did you have grandchildren? I have a couple, though I've never seen them...

I think my heart was beating harder than his that day after we pulled him out. I didn't even feel the mud, but I saw him vomit the water and mud out of him as we pounded him on his back...

I saved him, me and Rudy. I know this was the day Rudy decided to become a doctor. And I decided to stop the flooding.

Well, I tried, anyway. But you saved me, mamá. And because you saved me, I saved a little bit of the world, right? I did what I was supposed to do....

5

Con mucho cariño,
Tu Willie

Dear Vatos Locos, Brothers from the barrio, Good and Bad Men, Young Men especially (do they call you *homies* now?),

I think I'm gonna get mixed reviews for this letter, guys. I was a great son, a good brother, a loving father, a lousy husband. Sometimes I wish I could do it again...the thing is that if you're a man, you're not supposed to really love a woman unless you're weak, and I for sure wasn't that.

I had my share of fights. Won them all.

I ended up suing! Eighty-five times in Court over voting rights – and some people started calling me super-bad names, scared of me. Got sort of famous for this. Infamous.

But I'm really known for the time when I beat up the school bully. 1959. High School, Central Catholic. Picture this: I'm basically a nobody, a boy with thick glasses. The biggest white kid in the school is a terrorist in my book. Calls me names, cuts into the cafeteria line, pushes everyone around. Every school has one. This is the same year the Black college students in North Carolina were protesting segregation 'cause the white kids didn't want them. I guess this guy thought he had some power or something over me. Not many guys who were my kind of brown in that school.

Caab..n[3]. Oops, can't say those words in these letters according to the Big One. Anyway, you get the idea. Hear you have a President just like him now.   Well, me and the would-be terrorist met at Woodlawn Lake, and he was twice my size, and maybe two years older than me. I had been practicing. First rule: Prepare. I'd been training for weeks. Knew his weak spots. Second Rule: Focus. Focus some more. Rule:

---

[3] A common, elastic curse that is literally translated as "male goat," but means bad man, deceiving man, etc.

Don't miss, 'cause he's bigger than you...You might not get another chance.... They say I "destroyed" him. Everyone was there from the school and saw the whole thing. Then I was a hero alright.

All I had were my fists. And my moves. Third rule: When you throw a punch, aim, do it like you mean it. Then jump, cause he's always bigger. Fourth rule: Fly!! It's about the heart. You can do much more than you think if you have the spirit. Train. Focus. Jump.

I don't give up. Fly!

Learned so much that day. It was gonna be my first big fight as I got on with my life. And listen: Women? I never beat them up, but I never learned how to really listen to them, either. Train. Focus.... Did I ever mess up in that department...and I know it has to do with my father always being gone, the way he argued with my mother, the priests who said women couldn't run the Church like they did. And how my own mother cried all the time. How much she loved me, how she sacrificed for me to go to school, then college. This is all I knew about men and women.

Now I understand that if you don't have a father, you have to find your own way to be a man. It's not the gangs. Or the Church. Or even football. Or the Army. Sure didn't help my father.

It's in the books. That's one of the things mamá taught me.

How she loved me, and she told me all the time. This is more power than any bully's punch.

And later I had daughters, raised them to be strong, and I hope they are. My beautiful girls. I want the men in their lives to respect them. They better. I want to tell Janie, my wife, that I'm sorry. I'm so sorry.

But this is for another letter, not yet.

Listen guys, I want you to be a better man than I was. Defend yourself against bullies. A man defends. Remember the rules. And respect women, 'cause they will be mothers who will love you and this world so much, sometimes too much, but they make everything so beautiful. Don't be a bully with women and the people you love. And when you fall in love, apologize when necessary. And don't be afraid to cry. I should've cried more at night instead of drinking.

7

Yours in solidarity,
Willie

Dear All of You Who are Different, Lonely, and Definitely Not Most Popular:

Listen. Don't worry. I was different. Always was. Still am.

I was the guy nobody noticed. Too much Catholic in me. Too many problems at home, and always worried about my mother, my brothers and sister. My Mom and Dad fighting all the time.

Had to work all kinds of hours to pay my way through Catholic school and had no time for parties. I had to grow up fast. No sleep. When you're the oldest, you're in charge. Just the way it is. Plus, I looked like a nerd. Didn't have the good clothes, the attitude, the car, the looks. I was just – me. Girls didn't know I was alive and I didn't even try.

Because I worked all the time in high school at Central Catholic, I wasn't even a top student. Just average. Had a hard time with Latin, physics, chemistry and math. And they are so important, trust me! And I wasn't too good in religion, either. Asked too many questions.

But now, I give you an "A" if you're different. All those hard times, those lonely weekends, taught me that the world isn't what it seems. It's good to be different. You learn to be strong, brave, independent, cause you're the star *and* the audience. Yes, the world has a lot of suffering, and I'm not innocent about that. I was a messed-up kid for sure, but I learned that the world isn't about what you have, what you look like. The world is about what you do with what you have. Like having dreams. Life is about knowing that the world isn't fair. And it's not fair so that you and me can learn to make it fair, get that? On the day I graduated from high school, I'd already decided I would make the world pay attention to the different. The Brown. The poor, like me. The many who work so hard they sleep in class sometimes.

Give me an "A," because I believed I could do it. Only you are gonna have to finish what I started.

Yours forever and ever,
Willie

Dear St. Mary's University,

Thank you for accepting me into college despite the fact I was just an average student. Maybe you saw something in me. I was glad to be there and I got down to it. While I was studying in San Antonio, a lot of you-know-what was going on in the rest of the world. But I stayed focused on my studies, and it paid off. I graduated with honors on Sunday, May 29, 1966 with a degree in International Relations. My plan then was to get a Master's in Economics, and then go work as a diplomat based in Washington, D.C. I'd already spent two summers in D.C., interning with Congressman Henry B. González, I thought I had an idea about what to expect. I'd done well.

So, after I graduated, I went to D.C. to work for Henry B. for the third time. On the way back home, though, I became part of history.

I got off the plane in Austin, Texas after taking a flight from Washington D.C. and this happened:

It was Labor Day, 1966: Farmworkers and other marchers arrived in Austin. They had walked 321 miles for two months from the Rio Grande Valley all the way to the Texas capital in the middle of summer under the very-hot Texas sun. They just wanted a minimum wage. That was all. Just a minimum wage. But Gov. John Connally told the marchers they were not welcome. Told them no one would be there to greet them. Cesar Chavez was there. He led the protesters off the crossing and toward the Capitol. This was the day most Americans became aware of this *campesino humilde* from the vineyards of California. Senator Ralph Yarborough welcomed the protesters. A second group sent by MLK was there, too. Over 8,000 people gathered at the capital.

I was there. It was wild, thumping, holy. People were praying, holding on to each other.

There's nothing more patriotic than protest.

I was there. I was there. You have to listen to the signs, no matter what. And I did. Now do you see why I couldn't go back to Washington, D.C. to be a diplomat?

Respectfully,

Willie

THREE YEARS OF YOU-KNOW WHAT IN THE 60S

August 28, 1963: March on Washington
Martin Luther King gives his legendary "I have a Dream" speech.

September 15, 1963: Klu Klux Klan Bombs Birmingham Church
Four little girls die.

October 7, 1963: Freedom Day in Selma, Alabama
Black citizens are attacked at courthouse, prevented from registering to vote.

November 22, 1963: President John F. Kennedy assassinated
Gunman shoots, kills president during Dallas parade.

January 8, 1964: State of the Union address
President Lyndon B. Johnson calls for a War on Poverty.

January 23, 1964: The 24th Amendment passes
Poll Tax for federal elections is eliminated.

June 21, 1964: The Vietnam War begins
U.S. authorizes military action in Vietnam.

July 2, 1964: Civil Rights Act of 1964 passes
LBJ signs the Civil Rights Act, which bans segregation in all public places.

February 21, 1965: Malcolm X assassinated
Civil rights leader shot, killed during speech.

March 7, 1965: March to Montgomery begins
Protesters march to expose violence, oppression facing Black voters in the South.

August 10, 1965: The Voting Rights Act of 1965 passes
The Act outlawed discriminatory voting practices at the state and local level.

September 8, 1965: The Delano grape strike begins
Cesar Chavez leads farmworker labor strike against California, grape growers.

September 24, 1965: Affirmative Action passed into law
President Johnson issues an Executive Order

December, 1965: Farmworker labor strike gains national attention
Cesar Chavez sends farmworkers across the country to encourage national boycott.
Senator Robert Kennedy supports the grape boycott.

1966: U.S. troops in Vietnam rise to 400,000
Latinos serving in Vietnam disproportionate to their population in the U.S. College deferments are in effect.

11

Making my Dream Come True, Part 1

Dear Dreamers:

This is why I'm gone but not lost. Because of voting. Started to find myself. I was always working on voter registration drives when I was at St. Mary's University. My uncles, grandfather, and father, were all veterans. And still they struggled so much. They got no respect, despite their service. I didn't understand everything, but to me it was like fighting that bully – Train. Focus. Jump. So I started trying to get my barrio to vote for latino candidates who could help my uncles. Good jobs. More education. No flooding. You've seen voter registration drives, haven't you? This is when you go door-to-door with a clipboard and ask people if they have voted, and help them register to vote if they haven't.

Buenos días, are you registered to vote?
> *No I'm not interested.* (Slams door.)
Have a good day!

Buenos días, are you registered to vote?
> *Watch out for the dog, he bites!* (a pit bull comes running from the couch. A Chihuahua attacks. A German Shepherd smells you up....)
Buenos días, are you registered to vote?
> *I'm sorry, my husband votes in this house.* (Slams door.)

Buenos días, are you registered to vote?
> *I don't speak English.* (Slams door.)

Buenos días, are you registered to vote?
> *I can't man.... Just got out of Huntsville.* (He has lots of tattoos.)
> *Football game is on.* (Slams door, nicely.)

13

Then:

So you are registered to vote. Do you know where to go?
You don't know the candidates? You think they're all crooks?
Do you need a ride on that day?
You don't speak English? The registration card is bilingual. Voting is bilingual.
You don't believe in voting because you go to Church?
You're not a citizen yet after 20 years? 30? 50? Viva México?
Do you want a sign? What? You don't want to mess up your yard?
So, your husband takes care of this? Tells you how to vote?
Nothing will change?

The Big One's PA (Personal Angel) told me that we Latinos (we are not Hispanics anymore) accounted for half of the population growth in the U.S. between the elections of 2000 and 2004 but only 1/10 of the increase in the total votes cast.[4]

---

[4] Https://www.chron.com/opinion/outlook/article/Garcia-JFK-and-the-Latino-vote-4986092.php When President John F. Kennedy arrived in Texas on November 21, 1963, "he was on a particular political mission...his whole tragic trip to Texas was based on recapturing a momentum he once had with

WHEN WE WERE LOS CINCO

Dear Militants, Radicals *con Causa, Vanguardistas,* and Left-Bankers,

Okay, so I'm gonna tell it straight and real. There was another "*Los Cinco*", named after the Chicano political takeover in Crystal City, 1963.[5] You haven't learned about it yet? Look it up yourself: *Los Cinco,* Crystal City, Texas.

In short: Chicanos were like 80% of the population there but had no political representation. My college pal José Angel Gutierrez was involved in the organizing there, and "*Los Cinco*" took over – for a while, anyway.

But we were also called "*Los Cinco*" 'cause we were five militants, too, only we were all raising hell at St. Mary's University: me, José Angel, Mario, Nacho, and Juan.

There weren't many Mexicans at St. Mary's in those days. Much less Mexicans who came from the barrio; we had to work to get our tacos...so we recognized the signs in each other. Juan Patlán was the oldest, and he's the one who introduced me to José Angel[6]. José Angel was already the campaigner, being from Crystal City, where they'd made national news in 1963 when the Mexican-American slate won the majority seats there. Wow. Then there was Mario Compeán, who'd been a migrant

---

Mexican-American and Latino voters." Kennedy knew he needed Mexican-Americans if he was to have a shot at a second term. Ignacio M. Garcia, JFK & The Latino Vote, *Houston Chronicle,* November 16, 2013.

[5] The five San Antonio Chicano activists, including Willie Velásquez, who founded the Mexican-American Youth Organization (MAYO), were called Los Cinco after the Crystal City Activists.

[6] José Angel Gutierrez was from Crystal City, the capital of Zavala County in southwest Texas. He is considered by many to be the founder of La Raza Unida Party in Texas.

and was from the Westside projects, exactly the kind of guy my mother warned me against. Gutierrez already knew Juan Patlán, 'cause he was from Uvalde, and they had fought over the same girls while they were in college together. Ignacio "Nacho" Perez was the conceptual thinker. He was blunt, clear, not full of B.S.

We were smart guys, all five of us. Hard-working. It was the sixties and we were tired of the Texas Rangers and their violent history against us. We got no respect, not even the veterans. LULAC and the G.I. Forum were not militant enough for us. We became this study circle of five guys who studied and then went to meet them: Martin Luther King; Stokely Carmichael; Corky González; Cesar Chavez. Yeah, talk about field trips. We'd read about them, then get in a car over the weekend and go west, east, to Chicago – and meet these civil rights leaders.

You have to remember that in those days there weren't a lot of four-year colleges in South Texas. Just A&I in Kingsville.... The "talented tenth"[7] went to A&I in those days. I don't know why they let José Angel in there. Anyway, I met him when he transferred to St. Mary's graduate program in politics.

I'm not gonna lie. Part of the reason I joined them at Woodlawn Lake (a half-a-mile from St. Mary's), was because of the beer. You had to be 21 years old to buy it, and I didn't have money, anyway.... Patlán was older and was already working. Later, we went to the Fountain Room on Cincinnati. They let us in 'cause Patlán had the I.D....

I already knew Nacho Perez, who was deep in the farmworker struggle like I was. I brought him along. Nacho was the pensive

---

[7] The "Talented Tenth" is a term made popular by black thinker W.E. B. Du Bois, referring to a "leadership" class, or an "exceptional" class. "Los Cinco" were certainly this.

one. Compeán was the quiet one 'cause he stuttered. Patlán was steady, organized, kept records. Patlán was the diplomat. He stepped in just before I started to punch José in his big mouth one time.

Me and José? We talked and talked and argued and I never backed down. Let's just say that José Angel and I agreed on one thing only...we were both against the war. I think he was jealous of me 'cause I was just better-looking than him, let's face it. He had lost his father, a doctor, when he was twelve. He assumed that I had it made 'cause I had a father and never worked in the fields like he had to when his father died. Guess he was angry about everything that happened in his life, but I was angrier. I didn't have it easy, either.

We were not the same -- but we were all on the same page. Amazing.

José used to say that he had to be three people at once. The Perfect Gringo in school. The Perfect Mexican at home with his mother. That he could only be himself in the moment he left school and got home. During that time, he was a Chicano.

We all knew exactly how that felt.

This is called quantum synchronicity. Some people call it *El Destino*. Destiny.

I think it's just that we get these times when we meet people who are like people we've met before, people we didn't know existed but here they are. The chances of it all. It's special, once-in-a-lifetime.

It doesn't last. But those nights at Woodlawn with good cold beer, looking at the stars up there --- something happened. It was good, and it wasn't the beer talking, either. We found ourselves in each other.

And that's when we founded MAYO (the Mexican-American Youth Organization)[8] in 1967.

---

[8] MAYO, the Mexican-American Youth Organization, founded 1967, "was for a decade the major political organization of Mexican-American youth in Texas," Teresa Paloma Acosta, Texas State Historical Association (TSHA online).

Hope began in me under those stars. My dreams got big and bright as those stars.

It was magical dust we made, and I've never washed it off.

In brotherhood,

Willie

Making my Dream Come True, Part 2

THE SECRET TO GAINING POWER

Dear Dreamers:

Gonna tell you what it means to rule the world.

It's not about money (though that will come later). It's not about career or pleasing your parents cause they're not gonna like what I'm about to say.

The secret is: Follow your dreams. You want to be a comedian? A dancer? A football player?

You don't know what you want to do but you know what you love, dontcha? What would you do for free?

This is what you have to do...what you must do.

The secret is: If you do what you love, you will figure out what to do. Your "career" hasn't been invented yet. You have to create it on your own. It's not like I knew I was gonna be a voting rights pioneer when I was in high school – I thought I wanted to go to Washington D.C. and work in international relations. And I loved it. But I loved my barrio so much...so I ended up using everything I learned...I loved economics, I loved politics, I loved fighting. It all came together in getting my community their own leaders, and later, teaching them how to make those politicians respond to the people who elected them.

Voting matters when you want to buy a house. Medical care. The police. Water. Parks. Building universities in the barrio. The flooding – which was my big issue. And my community began to vote. And we did change some things for the better.

The secret is: It's not gonna be easy. I was poor till the day I was chosen by the Big One. But it didn't matter. I had done what I was supposed to do. I made waves. Not so much flooding in the barrio anymore, right?

19

The secret: Only do what you love. That's all that matters.
In brotherhood,
  Willie

Dear Dreamers:

During the time I was in college and hanging out with the other guys like me who wanted to change the world, here is how we changed it.

We created, established, built, started and organized and this is what we left behind for you:

1.   Mexican-American Youth Organization (MAYO), 1967

This was the first organization that came from us, "Los Cinco," and hanging out together. During the Spring Semester, we were all expelled for leafletting on behalf of the farmworkers. Nothing to fear when this happens. I was following my heart.

For a whole ten years, we were the major political organization for youth in Texas. We organized the walkouts, demonstrated in front of the Alamo, etc. Let's say we got attention.

And this was when foundations in New York were granting $$ for non-profit organizations targeting the Mexican-American communities (this was the sixties!), and how we learned about the 501(c)3 organization.

2.   Mexican-American Unity Council (MAUC), 1967

This was during the time that priests were very interested in social justice. This was the part of the Catholic Church I liked. And I became friends with Father Miguel Barragán, and together we formed a 501 (c)3 organization, just like we had been taught by the Ford Foundation. To improve conditions of the Latinos in the nation. But the Ford Foundation wanted to do more, and so we created:

3.   Southwest Council of La Raza, 1968

A regional organization that could take the lead in coherently organizing and funding Mexican-American community-building efforts
across the Southwest. It later became the National Council of La Raza.
Today it is UnidosUS, the country's largest non-profit Latino advocacy
organization, based in Washington, D.C. Works a lot on immigration
reform.

4.   LA RAZA UNIDA, 1970

La Raza Unida started as an alternative to the Democratic Party.
Experienced most of its success at the local level, when it helped sweep
local elections in Crystal City, Cotulla, and Carrizo Springs. Ramsey
Muñiz lost his bid for governor in 1972, but he obtained 6.28% of the
vote and scared the Democratic Party! La Raza Unida won fifteen local
positions in several borderland counties. It was happening! The Democratic Party never took us for granted again....

People will tell you that all this is s..t. That it ain't nothin. Not true!
I'm here – well not here – but I can verify that I was there, that I was
one of the founding members of all this, and that we shook up the
world. We really did.

How? Organize. Collaborate. Communicate. Establish your own.
Look it up. 501(c)3. A non-profit organization. Tax-exempt. You can
raise money, you can end up buying a building or land for what you
want to do. You don't have to work for anyone. You pick your board
who are your bosses, you pick your staff. You hustle like a maniac. I
sure did. This is very hard work – not gonna lie -- you have to keep
good records – obey the laws – but it's all worth it. You will be able to
save the world. I promise.

Forever,

Willie

Dear Big Dreamers:

It's always about representation, which comes down to voting.

You know where Lanier High School is? Right in the barrio in San Antonio, on the Westside. In 1968, there were demonstrations and riots all over the country. MLK was killed on April 4, 1968. Robert Kennedy was running for the presidency, and he would be killed in June. But nobody knew that yet, except maybe the Big One.

So now you know the atmosphere.

In March in East Los Angeles, nearly 22,000 Chicano students walked out of schools there to demand better curriculum so they could go to college instead of Vietnam or just vocational training. National news.

The Lanier High School students here were also demanding a college education, given that so many of the students were going

WALK OUT!

to Vietnam. And they couldn't even speak Spanish in school. Homer Garcia, a junior, brought up all these issues at a student council meeting, and was told to "shut up and sit down." He was interrogated, and asked if "communists were involved." Then he was expelled. The students began to organize a walkout.

Things got intense. Later, all the rebellious students were expelled. This was hard on the seniors, who were due to graduate in a few weeks. They came to MAYO, and I advised them. The students had serious demands. Met with Joe Bernal, then a State Senator, who had attended Lanier. He told them to organize, and that he needed to meet their parents.

After a lot of negotiations with teachers and administrators, things got even more heated.

County Commissioner Albert Peña was also meeting with the groups involved. Finally, about 700 parents, civic and religious leaders and activists got together in one meeting. After days of negotiation with the School Board, the SAISD Superintendent announced changes. Lanier would get college prep courses!

Homer ended up graduating from the University of Texas. Two master's degrees and a doctorate from Yale.

Edgewood High School was also protesting, which led to a class action lawsuit that changed Texas education funding policy forever. Bilingual education is available throughout Texas now. And all public school districts consider college goals as part of their student's time in the high schools.

Later in the year, the MAYO-supported protests went to the Valley, where maybe 150 students walked out of Edcouch-Elsa High School.

It's called the First Amendment. You can walk out! Even if you're in school. Just be prepared to be suspended or expelled. It's worth it. Now the principals are brown like me, but some are lost and I hope you're not.

Truly yours,

Willie

Dear Henry B. González[9], the Congressman who tried to punch me out,

You were like a father to me. I know I was like a son to you. You invited me to work in Washington, D.C. with you, and I helped you with your successful campaigns when I was at St. Mary's University.

We love you in San Antonio. You're like a God – the kind of God who stands up and defends us.

---

[9] Henry B. González. Henry Barbosa González, 1916 – 2000, was a Democratic politician from the 20th Congressional District of Texas from 1961 – 1999. He was known for his filibusters, fiery personality, and liberal views. He was in President Kennedy's motorcade through Dallas on November 22, 1963 when Kennedy was assassinated. González introduced legislation calling for the impeachment of Ronald Reagan and George H.W. Bush.

I wanted to be like you. It's just that I wasn't you – I was me. And I think you began to hate me when I began to find my own way that was different than you.

It began with that word, "Chicano." How could I not call myself that?

Black is beautiful. *Viva la Raza!* The American Indian Movement was rising up. Wounded Knee happened in 1973. They wanted their lands back. The gays in New York stood up at Stonewall in 1969. Right before I graduated from St. Mary's in 1965, 200,000 American soldiers arrived in Vietnam. There was a draft then, and all American men could be drafted. And they couldn't even vote for president! We resisted that war.

You see? This was my world. The veterans who returned from Vietnam were confused about why they had to be in that war, and after everything Mexican-Americans had to go through in Texas, we rose up. The boxing champ, Muhammad Ali, refused his draft to Vietnam, and they took away his titles in 1967.

> You wanted me to be
> a diplomat
> for a country
> that I could see was also
> **an empire.**

And though you were a Congressman and everything, and liked to fight too, excuse me, but you were born in 1916! You didn't have to go to Vietnam and didn't take it on...your parents were Mexican and came during the Mexican Revolution. I think you saw yourself as Mexican, but my uncles, father and grandfather were in World War I, World War II, Korea. My brother Ralph was in Vietnam. You were re-elected seventeen times in the 20th Congressional District. We were supposed to go to a war that had nothing to do with us. Why should we die for that?

Compared to my life, yours was easy. You were born in San Antonio too, but you graduated from Jefferson High School in the thirties. That was a middle-class white school. You weren't that poor. Is that how you made it through college? Law school? I didn't have any-thing, I'm not from the middle-class. I had to work every day.

Still, I know you suffered, and I know you believed in me. But I want to be a Texan, an American, on my terms. You came from a time when you had to be white to be treated with respect. I want respect for being me, that's all. You wanted me to be a diplomat for a country that I could see was also an empire, and I wanted to make it a democracy. I want my community to vote. Had figured out we could make things better this way. It's not unpatriotic to vote. I didn't want any more of my buddies to die so America could have more power in the world.

Democracy. I want to teach other countries that word, how to rule themselves through democracy. So, I call myself a Chicano. Is that so bad? Cesar Chavez used this word and he organized farmworkers throughout the Southwest and got this country to regulate pesticides, got more toilets – he got people to pay attention to the conditions of the people who pick our lettuce, tomatoes, and onions that we like in our tacos. Simple as that.

What do you have against them? I was never a farmworker, but I like to eat. Don't you?

Anyway, you came after me 'cause I supported the Farmworkers. Especially because of La Raza Unida. Called me a troublemaker. Sent the FBI and the CIA after us! Los Cinco[10] was too many besides you? What, wasn't San Antonio big enough for all of us?

All because we didn't, wouldn't, follow your standard of defending the "neglected people." How were we gonna change things if we didn't

---

[10] The name of the founders of the Mexican-American Youth Organization (MAYO); five Chicano activists, based in San Antonio, Texas – including Willie Velásquez.

vote and change the laws? Did you think you could do it all by yourself with your filibusters and your fists?

It's over, Henry B. It's over for me, too. I forgive you. You did your best.

Like I told Janie, you always voted right. Ok?

That's why I'm writing this letter. Someone out there is gonna read this, and then they will tell me to step aside.

Ok, I will. But I'm still a Chicano.

Viva La Raza,

Willie

Dear Janie, my wife and mother of my children,

I remember.

It was in May '69, right before your birthday, and I ran into you at the Garcia party.

You were at that protest in Del Rio, right? I think that's where we first met. You were a VISTA volunteer, and I, representing MAYO as one of its founders, was one of the 2,000 March leaders. The governor and the city's leaders sure didn't like VISTA. Senator Ted Kennedy sent a letter supporting us. It was all about voting education, but the world just saw hippies and trouble-makers. There were Catholic priests with us, members of the Texas state legislators, and even Dr. Hector P. Garcia, the founder of the veterans-based G.I. Forum. We all wanted to keep VISTA and Minority Mobilization workers in Valverde County. Congressman Henry B. González called us communists, and it only got worse from there. José Angel Gutierrez, went off as he tended to do and said things like "we have been oppressed for too long," blaming all the gringos, which made us look racist. So regular people thought we were communists and racists too.

Years later, I was quoted as saying that the Del Rio March was "the most significant march and demonstration by Chicanos in Texas history."

What I didn't say was why. It was "significant" because you were there, you, Janie Sarabia from Hutchinson, Kansas, with the gleaming long hair, *morena clara* skin, big eyes and bigger smile. Bell bottoms and peasant blouse that you wore better than any model. You told me you grew up as a migrant worker all your life, and I could see the fields, the cotton, and all the states you'd picked in behind the smile. You were a branch of a mesquite tree that nobody could cut down, its roots digging deep into San Antonio.

I met you there, protesting with me, and thought I'd never see you again.

Tu Willie

Dear Janie, my wife and mother of my children,

We met in May, 1969. Married a year later. I was barely 26, and you were 23. I was grown-up handsome by then and looked good in my tux with bow tie. You wore a fancy wedding dress. Pura traditional girl. God, we were in love!

I don't know where to begin with so many apologies I have to make to you. It's been thirty years since I've gone, but I still remember.

Our first dance at the Garcia's party was to Sunny & the Sun-liners[11], remember? I was watching the way you dance, I'm good at that because of my baseball days, and could see that you moved like a dancer from all those years working the fields.

Then I asked you to dance. It felt right. I touched your hands and almost fell from the electricity between us. Never happened before.

---

[11] Formed in San Antonio as Sunny & the Sunglows in 1959, this popular band achieved national stardom with its unique music style known as "Tejano (or Chicano) Soul".

Put me in jail. The Pony. Mashed Po-
tato. The Swim. The Jerk. I told you I
could play the accordion, and you con-
fessed you loved conjunto music. And
could you dance a *polkita.* As good as
American Bandstand on Tejano polkas.
Little Joe, Conjunto Bernal, you knew all
the steps forward and back, going round
fast with me, breaking out into rock-n-roll,
una cumbia, the roach-killer *guapango,* and
even Mambo #8 when they surprised us.
All the girls wearing mini-skirts but no one
looked as good as you in yours...*and then the judge accused me, he put
me down real bad, said that I was guilty of making you so sad.*

Put me in jail, Janie. I'm sorry, Janie. I'm sorry I talked you into
marrying me, seducing you with my college degree and everything I
would never really have. You gave me your all, and it was never
enough. I wanted to change the world and you wanted that too, but
you also believed in love, even when I loved the world and forgot about
you.... You never laughed when I told you my dreams, but I put you
down real bad sometimes...just didn't know what it would cost us.

Tu Willie

MAKING MY DREAM COME TRUE, PART 3

HOW TO GET POWER

Dear Dreamers:

When you are searching, the universe is searching for you, too. I have come to understand that things happen in ways you can't plan exactly, but they will happen if you know what you have to do in the world.

I realize now there aren't many like me. You know why they call me a "hero?" Only because I did what I was supposed to. And I did it even when I couldn't afford a taco. Didn't matter. My brother, bless you, George, always got me one when I called him. He always understood me.

I miss you, George. *Hermano, de veras.*

By 1974, which was like eight years after college, and maybe seven years after dropping out of my master's program at St. Mary's, I was broke, married to my beautiful Janie, and had a baby daughter, Carmen.

I'd been working with the Southwest Council of La Raza, which I helped found – in 1968 - one of those non-profits that was serving the community through advocacy (speaking out for their rights), mostly. Not much money in it, but I loved the work.

Here's the thing: the SCLR board and me really wanted to set up a Mexican-American voter registration organization. This was in the years right after the Voting Rights Act of 1965, and we wanted to see more Latinos and Latinas participate in the system.[12]

---

[12] Signed into law by President Lyndon B. Johnson (Texas). Landmark legislation that prohibits racial discrimination in voting.

It was so hard. President Nixon didn't want to see non-profits like ours receive funding from foundations or labor unions for voting purposes—he realized that most of us vote "Democrat."

Congressman Henry B. González was still upset with me because of MAYO, calling myself a Chicano, turning down a diplomat's job in D.C., and raising hell all over the place, so we didn't have a lot of support. We had to work with very little money and paid close attention to African-American voter registration efforts, especially VEP, the leading Black voter registration organization in the South.[13]

By 1971, the Southwest Council of La Raza created CVREP, as the Citizen Voter Research Education Project. We were denied three times by the IRS. There is no way you can be tax exempt without getting 501(c)3 status, and you can only get 501(c)3 status through the IRS. The president had the power to stop us.

Yes, we were trying to get people to vote. And many of those people might one day vote against the conservative president and about them, really. 'Cause Democrats have also made lots of mistakes in the past. What it's about is DEMOCRACY.

I just believed that my community really needed to understand this idea – which is much bigger than any president. It's about justice and equality for all – and how everyone – no matter how rich, poor, disabled, old or young. You name it. Everyone deserves a right to belong and participate. This will keep us living together through good and bad

[13] Founded during the Civil Rights period. The Voter Education Project as an Atlanta based voting rights and voter education organization that worked in the Southern United States from 1962-1968.

times. We are individuals, yes, but we are also a nation of people who have to get along in order to help each other be the best they can be. Democracy.

We were rejected by the IRS three times after 5 ½ years of trying. But I don't give up. I formed a new organization and called it the Southwest Voter Registration and Education Project, based out of Texas. SVREP. And this one passed because I don't give up!

I was thirty years old. And the organization's address was at my house in San Antonio. It was 1974.

Forever and ever,

Willie

.

Making my Dream Come True, Part 4

YOUR VOTE IS YOUR VOICE / SU VOTO ES SU VOZ

Dear Dreamers:

How can I explain how I found my voice? What is it? It's how you talk, how you move, what makes you laugh, where you come from.

It's nothing to be ashamed of. It's your power.

The writers I knew told me once that the world-class writers all understood this. That once you realize you don't have to write like Shakespeare, you're home-free.

That's when I realized that I don't have to be like MLK or Kennedy or even Gandhi. I studied these guys, but I was me. They were in me, just like the barrio was in me.

That's when I found my voice. I spoke like St. Mary's had taught me. But I also spoke like my friends from the projects who my mother tried to keep me away from. Some people call them "*gente baja,*" but they're not. They are me, and I'm not a low-life. I'm a high-life 'cause I am all I've seen and know and speak out loud.

My voice is comfortable everywhere. My voice speaks many languages – English, Spanish, Tex-Mex, etc., and that's a good thing. I refuse to be ashamed of who I am.

My voice is my power. And once I began to understand all this, I saw that voting is our voice wanting power in our way. Representing. Respectful. Understanding that the poorest people many times are also the richest because they share everything they have with you. There's nothing like the beans your mother makes you with all her love. Or your grandmother's *empanadas de calabasa.* How can this be poor?

When I started registering people to vote, I told them: *su voto es su voz*. Your vote is your voice.

This really means: I'm voting for someone who respects me for who I am. And who's gonna work for me day and night.

Su voto es su voz. Your vote is your voice. Democracy.

Willie

Making my Dream Come True, Part 5

FOLLOW YOUR TRIPAS: HOW TO GET POWER

Dear Dreamers:

It was always the flooding that called me. 1913. 1921. 1935. 1965. 1972. 1987. People died every time. And I wasn't there, but I watched: 1994. 1998. 2002. 2013. 2015. And this is just the San Antonio area, there have been other floods all over Texas, and of course, Houston in 2017 because of Hurricane Harvey. (We have The Big One radio here).

I love my city of San Antonio built on a river.[14] And the creeks that make up a fine, fine thread of embroidered wet in my barrio. San Antonio has water, and that's why we're so green we're blue-green in the Spring. There's nothing like going to the creek and listening to the frogs, listen to the way the wind speaks when the breeze comes in late at night in the summer. I love the mushiness that the water brings, everything sparkles more, especially the smell of fresh water after a good rain cause it's like a newborn day every time. There is a smell to green, you know what I mean? The bougainvillea bring us their hot pink flirt, the orange trees have the perfume alongside the romance of jasmine, but it's the water that always made my heart dance. I could see myself, the little fish and ducks and butterflies and even the scary snakes, in the water. Life. I felt like I was part of the water, too. It calmed me. It made me happy. It belonged to me, too.

---

[14] Considered by many to be one of the most soulful and haunted cities in Texas – home to the Alamo, and to a vast network of creeks and rivers that served the dozens of indigenous communities that lived there. San Antonio was named for St. Anthony of Padua by the Spaniards. Founded in 1718.

But those floods. I learned in college that cities are designed by the people in power, and that a city like ours needs some serious planning for what's called drainage. And you need dams. So, when the rains hit the river and the creeks, the overflow can rush into drains that take the water eventually to the ocean. Back home in San Antonio, it was the poorest people who lived by the downtown river, and we were at the lowest level, so the water from the rains on the Northside really hit us hard. No one seemed to care what happened every time it rained. And it rains a lot here. It would cost big money.

Rains mean destruction here. Not beauty. Not romance. Rains mean mud. Mosquitoes. Houses falling down. People drowning.

I decided that I was gonna change all this. But how?

Voting.

Forever,

Willie

Making my Dream Come True, Part 6

HOW TO GET POWER FROM THE CHUPA-CABRAS

Dear Dreamers:

Why don't we have power? Because we don't vote, simple as that. The Constitution says you can vote if you're a citizen, 15th Amendment. Women got the right with the 19th Amendment.

And some of us vote alright.

Here's the trick: Not enough of us vote, that's the problem.

Here's another trick: We have to really like the person who's running. A person who we can identify with in some way. This is called representing.

Next trick. We have to get into the system of precinct chairs, party elections and conventions.

The biggest mind-trick: Gerrymandering. Voting maps. Who represents your area, and why? How does this happen? People who run your city, state, and the country, draw the maps. They design the maps so that certain communities are weakened, diluted, 'cause they know that if enough of us vote we can change things. So their guy or lady wins. Simple as that. Gerrymandering cases are in the courts rights now. All over the place.

We, SVREP, sued 85 times over these maps. And 85 times we won. Bullies, that's what they are. Gerrymandering is ruled by all kinds of *chupacabras*.

Remember: TRAIN. FOCUS. JUMP.

It was the research preparation that did it. Train.

With my lawyers[15] (you call them peeps), working round-the-clock and for almost nothing, we found seventy rural counties in Texas with signs of "systematic weakening of the Mexican-American vote."[16]

Too many. Focus.

Here are two of the *chupacabras* we battled on our way to getting some representation so that our votes could count. And what they said about the Southwest Voter Registration & Education Project (SVREP), Mexican-American Legal Defense Educational Fund (MALDEF), Rural Legal Aid, private lawyers, and others with voting rights experience. (It takes a barrio, doesn't it?)

In Mathis, Texas we represented "big government".
In west Texas, they called us "agitators".
They called us "traitors to their country and the Catholic faith".
They called us "communist-inspired"
Uh-huh...and this is what I can print.

Why does voting matter? Higher minimum wage jobs. Public schools. The prison system. The police. Housing. Taxes. Believe me, everyone votes in Westchester County, one of the richest counties

---

[15] Willie's lawyers included Joaquín Ávila of MALDEF and SVREP's Roland Rios.

[16] Sepúlveda, Juan A. Jr., *The Life and Times of Willie Velásquez*, Arte Público Press, 2003.

(upstate New York) in the country...I've seen it myself. Rich people vote. And they put up signs in their beautiful yards.

Those who win the election are the ones who make these decisions.

So, if you want to keep people from voting:

1. Make it hard work. Make it cost. Charge a poll tax. Require a driver's license, an ID card. Make them get a new registration card every time they move.

2. Make people pass tests.

3. Schedule voting so that people can't get to the voting place when they're working.

4. Don't tell people where they are supposed to go vote. Make it crazy.

5. Make sure the newspapers and radio and television don't talk much about it.

6. If all this doesn't work, then draw the voting maps into a psycho puzzle–through *chupacabra* "gerrymandering" and/or redistricting, from Congress to city councilmen and women, to the schoolboard elections, so that people don't have a chance to win an election in their own community, because the map is drawn to include more middle-class people or people who are not gonna vote for your candidate no-matter-what.

7. Make it super-expensive for someone to win an election.

8. And if all this doesn't work, then bribe the candidate so that he or she falls apart with greed. It happens.

Make people give up with all this B.S.

Me, I was just interested in the flooding in San Antonio in my barrio. I wanted to stop it.

Forevers,

Willie

Chupacabra Gerrymandering in Texas

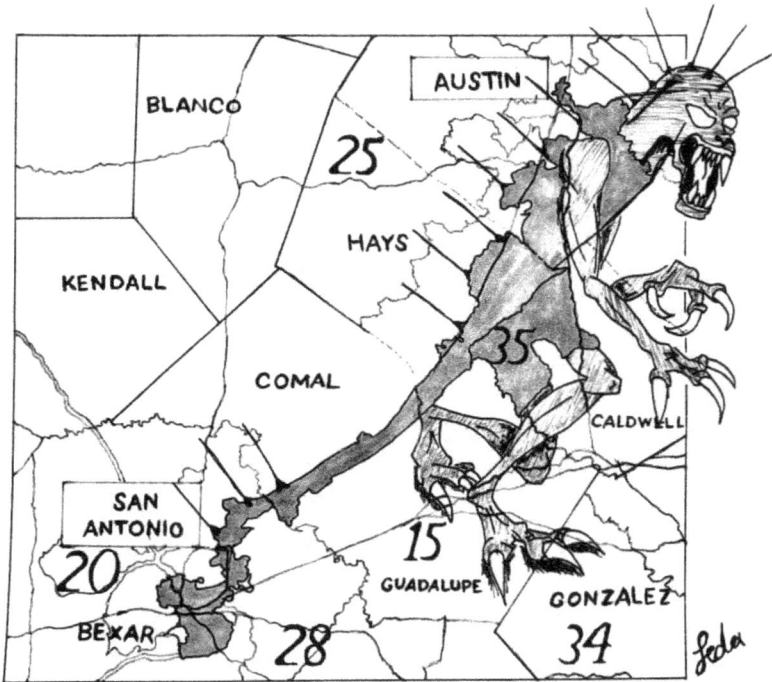

Making my Dream Come True, Part 7

HOW TO GET POWER DESPITE THE *CHUPA-CABRAS*[17]

Dear Dreamers:

Let me tell you about the Jones case in Lubbock, Texas. 1983.

This was our first at-large challenge.

A community leader named Eliseo Solis ran for County Commissioner. He did everything right – door-to-door campaigning. He beat the Anglo contenders in the Primary election. Then he lost by 107 votes to one of the Anglos in the runoff! He found evidence of suspicious irregularities at the county courthouse. Cheating stuff. When they complained to one of the county election officers, they were told that the book of elections law did not apply to "Mexicans."

Hispanics at the time made one-quarter of the total population, yet they had no representation whatsoever. Why? Because they had to get the votes from all over the city instead of their particular neighborhoods. They could never win this way. Train.

---

[17] Literally, "goat-sucker." A legendary, mythical, creature that attacks and drinks the blood of livestock. It has been seen in Puerto Rico and throughout the world, but especially in the Texas Southwest and along the U.S.-Mexico border.

The SVREP lawyers and the researcher Bob Brischetto were able to show that most Anglos did not vote for Mexican-Americans or Blacks (This is why you train!). Focus.

The judge agreed! The judge found overwhelming proof that the elected officials of Lubbock were administering an electoral system that was fundamentally unfair to its minority citizens.

Jones vs. The City of Lubbock was big-time! It was the first successful at-large case tried under the newly amended Voting Rights Act.

And by April 1983, a Mexican-American and an African-American were elected to the Lubbock City Council *for the first time* in the city's history, thanks to the new single-member districts that came out of *Jones vs. City of Lubbock*.

Jump. Jump! What comes after this?

FLY! The Corpus Christi school district went to single-member districts right after, and a few weeks after that, it was the Beeville ISD.

Fly.

Willie

Making my Dream Come True, Part 8

TRAIN. FOCUS. JUMP. FLY.

Dear Dreamers,

But all this was just the beginning. I knew by then that anywhere there were 30-40% "Hispanics" or African-Americans, and that they didn't have political representation, we could address it. And that my community would vote.

Now for stage two of the plan. (Focus).

The voting maps. That word, gerrymandering. How to fight once you know the game? You need the A-Team. Gotta be better. In my case, that meant lawyers. I found them, and paid them what I had, which was almost nothing. But they became some of the best lawyers in the country in the field of voting rights. I'm proud of them.

Remember:

1. **TRAIN.** This was all our research, data-driven, so we knew the subject better than anyone else. This is why you need college and the best professors.

2. **FOCUS.** I knew SVREP had to get lawyers for the gerrymandering. The research showed me that getting people to vote wasn't enough if they couldn't elect their own because of gerrymandering and at-large districts.

3. **JUMP.** Let's get it on in court.

4. **FLY.** Make our new elected officials responsible.

Forevers,

Tu Willie

43

Dear Henry Cisneros[18],

It was 1981. I'd been married more than 10 years and had three kids – Carmen and Cata and Guillermo was around four years old. Janie's father had died in 1978, and we were really struggling. Then you, Henry, decided to run for mayor.

Henry, you knew that you benefitted from the Chicano activists in the city, even though many of us had questions about your commitment to Mexican-American neighborhoods. I had tried to convince you not to run for City Council in 1975 under the Good Government League banner (GGL). These were the whites who had held equality back for so long. I tried to urge you to rely on the Southwest Voter Registration & Education Project (SVREP) for the city-wide voter registration and education drive you were gonna need.

Not just the White or Anglo vote. Or the gringo vote, as Gutierrez liked to call it.

Henry. You had more faith in the GGL than us.

We were so proud of you, I still am. We knew that your election would help all of us, and that was enough for us to support you even if we didn't agree with your careful and considered ideas. You even spoke like you'd been in a Shakespeare debate. We knew your father was a former colonel, that you graduated from A&M, and we forgave you for being socialized like you were better than us. We understood.

The SVREP staged a 4-week registration drive followed by a voter education effort. There were other candidates, too, in other races. We wanted people to understand who they were voting for and to make them accountable. We registered thousands of people to vote. You won the race! SVREP showed a much higher turnout rate than either whites or African-Americans!

---

[18] Cisneros served as the mayor of San Antonio, Texas, from 1981 – 1989. He was the second Latino mayor of a major American city, and the first Latino mayor since 1842. President Clinton appointed him to his Cabinet as Secretary of Housing and Urban Development (HUD), where he served from 1993-1997.

You received nearly 95% of the Mexican-American vote.

You also got nearly 40% of the white vote with some districts giving you nearly half of the total votes cast. And 75% of the black vote. Wow!

Of course, it was you. But I know you know we helped in getting the vote out. And we didn't make it easy for you when you made history and became the first Mexican-American Mayor of San Antonio since Juan Seguín in 1842 (and he was forced out). At that time, we were the tenth-biggest city in the country.

Henry, you put San Antonio on the map. As a councilman, thank you for working with Ernie Cortés and COPS (Communities Organized for Public Service), a grassroots advocacy group that brought development funding into the barrios and helped control the worst flooding.[19]

And in 1977, in a vote that changed your life and ours, four years before you became Mayor, you voted to accept an election plan by the Justice Department for single-member districts, which meant that Mexican-Americans were finally gonna get a voice in government!

(Thank you, Professor Charles Cotrell, for showing me the way!)

This led to the fading of the GGL, and maybe that's why you knew you had to work with us too, and that they could only help you and not hurt you.

So, you were mayor from 1981 – 1989. And while I didn't always agree with you, I am proud that SVREP worked to get people to vote. The work we did in San Antonio was our eighth voter registration campaign. After it was over, we had increased voter registration of Mexican-Americans (and Latinos as you call them now) from 40,000 to 153,000 voters that year. Pretty good, huh?

Now don't let us down ever again, ok? I'm not around, but I'm watching you, Henry.

---

[19] A premier labor organizer from San Antonio, Cortés in 1974 founded Communities Organized for Public Service (COPS), the nationally-recognized Church-based grassroots organization of San Antonio's Westside and Southside communities.

Hasta the next taco,
Willie

Dear San Antonio,

I did it for her.

From 1981 – 1988, seven years left. I didn't know that then.

Before I tell that story and what happened, gonna tell you why.

People will tell you I was a voting rights "champion." Or "pioneer." Wrong.

It's true that my organization, the Southwest Voter Registration & Education Project (SVREP), held over 1,000 voter registration drives in the Southwest (whew!) and that we were essential in increasing the Latinos registering to vote to almost 5 million! All by 1988. When the Big One said, *come here.*

With so many more of us voting, things changed a lot. We went from 1500 Latino elected officials in 1974 – to 3300 elected officials by 1988. Of course, the 85 lawsuits we won helped. You get one success, and the rest of the counties get scared and start negotiating.... The San Antonio redistricting victory in 1977 also contributed—it sure helped Henry Cisneros as a councilman when he only had to run from one district, from his barrio, instead of "at large," all over the city.

Single-member districts means that each "district" gets their own councilperson or representative. It wasn't always this way. Trust me, it's a lot easier to serve your barrio and get popular this way than covering the whole city! This is why we need single-member districts.

Back to my point.

I, Willie Velásquez, was a lover...of democracy. Voting and the lawsuits were just a way to get there.

Let me explain.

I was all about democracy. Hate to say it, but there is good and bad in all people. How do you balance it? I did it for her. Lady Liberty. She has faith in us, and I am in love with her. She has a light touch in

46

all the shouting and screaming. If you don't read the rest of my letters, understand this.

Forevers,
Willie

Dear San Antonio,

Free Speech is me.

Don't you want to speak when you are burning up with something to say? Free speech, press, religion, assembly (peaceful), 1st Amendment.

Don't you want a way to defend yourself if someone wants to burn your house down or something? The 2nd Amendment. The right to bear arms to defend yourself and your property.

P.S. Women aren't property. (And dogs–shouldn't be).

There's ten of them – all great. Others include:

13TH AMENDMENT – ABOLISHED SLAVERY

15TH AMENDMENT – THE RIGHT OF CITIZENS TO VOTE

19TH AMENDMENT – RIGHT OF WOMEN TO VOTE

26TH AMENDMENT – RIGHT TO VOTE FOR CITIZENS AT AGE 18

There are countries in this world where you can't travel without a permit. Or leave. There are countries in this world where you can't go out to the public square and challenge the leaders or the police. You might end up in prison – for life if you say anything negative about the president. There are countries in the world where you can vote–but it doesn't mean anything. The votes are always broken into or manipulated. So, the president becomes a dictator for life.

A democracy like ours is different. That's why so many want to come here. We can speak out. We can protest. We can vote the corrupt out. All of this makes families stable, and then they want an education so they can get ahead. We have impeached a president. And we had a civil rights movement, like when I was growing up, that got us out of Vietnam, finally.

We're no better than anyone else, we're just a democracy. And that's pretty messy with everybody yelling all at once. The rich still want to get richer, and the poor don't understand their own power in a democracy. But I did, and I used it to stop the flooding.

And it was hell. But it worked. Voting is like yelling so everyone hears you for sure. And if there's enough voting, then you change the world.

Yours truly,
Willie

Dear San Antonio,

Why I'm not much of a hero:

A hero challenges the "status quo," the establishment. I did plenty of that. Train. Focus. Jump.

I had moves alright. And I wasn't afraid, either. A hero learns something during his (or her) adventure out there and brings the lessons home, to the people.

What lessons did I learn?

GOOD:

That you can do more than you can imagine. That doing also includes being a good person.

BAD:

I yelled at everybody and hurt their feelings.

GOOD:

That dreams begin to come true as you start talking about them.

BAD:

Maybe I was willing to pay the price for my dreams, but I also made Janie and my children pay, too.

GOOD:

That when I knew what my purpose was, nothing could stop me.

48

BAD:

Even if it meant I wasn't gonna go to any family parties, or watch my son play soccer. I'm so sorry, *mijo*.

A real hero is supposed to come back home with the flame of truth in his hand. Well, here's my letters. Only took 30 years.

A real hero is humble. Listens. Patient. Not me! I think that's what made me sick....

So, do you think this is hero behavior? Looking back, I could've done better. Guys, if you have dreams, get married and share the dream. Include your wife and family in everything, 'cause they probably want to help. Ladies, if you have dreams, don't get married. Janie had dreams too, and I didn't have room for hers like she had for mine. I'm sorry, Janie.

I was so tired by this time. That's when I got invited to teach at Harvard.

Tu Willie

Dear San Antonio,

Harvard. Invited. Wow.

It was only for a semester, but for me it was one of my biggest dreams coming true. Like living in Shakespeare culture, but it's modern. Lots of brains walking around. Libraries from the Gods! Bookstores on every block. The subway. Music, like classical, everywhere. Musicians playing on the streets. The American Revolution and the statues. And I'd always wanted to write a book on Chicano politics and organizing....

I was finally legit, not some nobody with no money raising hell all over the Southwest. Harvard wanted me to teach what I'd learned about Chicano politics! And I could hang out with the professors whose books I'd studied, and we could talk late into the night and compare their research with how things really were in the barrio. They were interested in me, us, and I needed what they'd learned for SVREP.

Janie was not thrilled about any of this — too much work for her with the three kids in school, since I was rarely home. She brought her mother, too. Had very little time for sightseeing, and there is plenty to see there. A public aquarium. The Boston Tea Party history and everything. Cape Cod where the Kennedys live. Lobster in Maine. Boston is a walkable city, really. But it was lonely for her. We ended up in a tiny apartment and then she left me and took the kids and her mother, deciding to go to her first home in Kansas.

Part of me missed my family. Part of me was finally at peace. What can I say?

Okay, so I was alone at Harvard. You know what that's like? Lots of rich people from all over the world. The kind of people who take their Spring Break in Europe, not Padre Island. The kind of people who know at least two languages, usually three or more, and are proud of it. And me. Lots of nerds. The children of presidents, senators, judges, and the children of dictators and drug lords. I'm serious. Expensive. No matter. I fit in real well there since they saw me as leading a voting revolution in the Southwest. I wore my guayabera under my coat at all times, very cool.

I hung out with the Greek crowd while I was there. They're just like us. Immigrants. Proud. Welcoming.

I was happy there.

Afterwards I drove to Kansas and picked up my family. I'm sorry, Janie.

El Willie

Making My Dream Come True, Part 9

HOW TO GET POWER EVEN WITH A CHUPA-CABRA PRESIDENT

Dear San Antonio,

First, the good news. Cause I also have bad news. I returned from Harvard, alright, and got to work. Spring, 1983.

Five more years till the Big One called me. Didn't know that at the time. I did feel the clock, ticking, ticking real loud, for sure. Had to get things done!

Surprise. SVREP was getting some respect around the country. The foundations, and they have zillions of dollars compared to me, were inviting me to speak about voting education. Part of this was because the presidential election of 1984 was coming. And the progressives in the country wanted to take the White House back from Reagan, who was president. I think the most liberal foundations realized they had to get involved in "minority empowerment," yet they were still nervous about it getting too politicized because Reagan and his administration were watching them closely.

These foundations, part of the national movement, thought of SVREP, VEP, and Operation Big Vote, as essential in the national mobilization of voters. SVREP was the leader among the Latino (we called it Hispanic) voter education projects. The others I mentioned were African-American.

I was inspired by their attention. I could see that these kinds of funders were beginning to see that minority participation was critical to American democracy! We just had to vote and participate in the democratic process at all levels.

But it turned out to just be a moment.

SVREP began to get some serious funding. Especially for the research work (Train). Voter education, or field organizing, as we called it, was second priority (Focus). And it was very hard to get funding for the lawyers – or litigation (Jump).

But I don't give up. Not me.

Then President Ronald Reagan came to San Antonio. Why? Because he knew that he needed our vote 'cause we were voting and challenging gerrymandering and moving into single-member districts. We showed up on his radar, that's why. He had to pay attention to us.

He came for Cinco de Mayo. Henry Cisneros was there. It was a happening. Did you miss it?

El Willie

Making my Dream Come True, Part 10

How to Get Power in the Time of *Chupacabras*

Dear Dreamers,

1984. Four years left. Hadn't figured it out yet, but who does?

It was time to step up our game. I decided to organize a national event of our own. A voter promotion blow-out. Here in San Anto. This way, no one—no one—could doubt that we counted.

I guess I was trying to make the national politicians responsible. So we made all kinds of predictions, projections, and set a new standard for minority Latino (I know, not Hispanic) participation.

The VIPs from around the country showed up: Mayor Henry Cisneros. Dr. Blandina Cárdenas. Raul Yzaguirre. Tony Bonilla, president of LULAC (League of United Latin American Citizens). Harry Pachón, Director of NALEO (the National Association of Latino Elected Officials). Los Angeles Deputy Mayor Grace Montañez. And many others; you get the picture.

The goal: to increase the number of Latino registered voters in the United States by one million individuals. From 3.4 million – to 4.4 million by November of 1984!

Democrats and Republicans had a stake in this. And the more we voted, the more we became critical to the "swing" votes, which could decide key elections. Train.

We wanted R.E.S.P.E.C.T. Did we get there?

No.

Dear San Antonio,

By this time, SVREP had conducted more than 500 voter registration campaigns since it began to fly in 1974.

I knew (TRAIN!) that Latinos had been the critical swing vote in Governor Mark White's election in Texas. Governor Toney Anaya in New Mexico. Chicago's Mayor Harold Washington in 1983. Without us, they would have lost, pure and simple.

Then Vice President George Bush came to visit in late 1983. (You know him as "Daddy" Bush). This was the climax of our voter registration campaign that we'd initiated. The Republicans were really, really trying for our vote.

I got a chance to hang out with Bush in the limousine. I shared our research regarding bilingual education. Ninety-three percent of us want it, I told him. He was open to this, said it made sense. He did not have a problem that the Reagan Administration supported it, and he said so that night. I helped him add this to his speech.

"Let me make this crystal clear – we are for bilingual education...Good bilingual programs make it possible to phase into the English-speaking mainstream." That's what he said, and I helped him write it.

Well, I speak Spanish and English, so you can too, right?

But this wasn't the best part. All kinds of Latino elected officials were there talking about the vote and SVREP.

Senator Ted Kennedy made a speech. Cesar Chavez introduced him – who was the most respected Latino leader in the country.

Cesar took on the Republican administration. Reminded them how Richard Nixon and Reagan had purposefully eaten grapes on television.

Kennedy also blasted the Republicans. He said that he was "less concerned about whether the president eats Mexican food and more concerned about the Mexican-American families who don't have enough to eat."[20]

By the time all the hoopla was over, SVREP knew we had our work cut out for us. We were gonna work it through the Southwest: California; Texas; Arizona; Colorado; New Mexico, and eight other states. Midwest Voter Registration & Education Project (MWVREP) was gonna register through the Midwest: Illinois, Ohio, Michigan, Indiana, and Wisconsin, among other states. They'd already had some successes. Then there was the Puerto Rican Coalition that wanted to take on New York, Massachusetts, New Jersey, Pennsylvania, and Connecticut. This was collaboration all right.

Did we make our goals of a million new voters?

No. Not even close.

But we won in other ways.

Willie

---

[20] "I am less concerned about whether the president eats Mexican food and more concerned about the Mexican-American families who don't have enough to eat." - Senator Robert Kennedy, *The Life and Times of Willie Velásquez,* by Juan A. Sepúlveda, Jr., Arte Público Press, 2003.

MAKING MY DREAM COME TRUE, PART 11

HOW TO GET POWER IN THE TIME OF CHUPACABRAS

Dear Dreamers:

So how do you win when you lose?

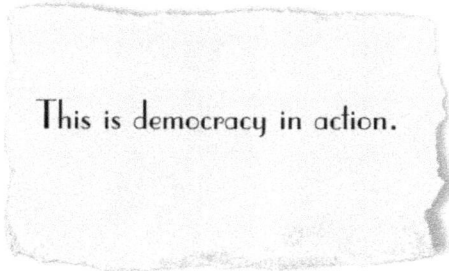

SVREP learned how to build coalitions. How to be a team player. How to share, that's how. We supported voter registration efforts in Filipino-American communities in California. With Chinese-Americans in San Francisco. African-Americans in Houston, that's how. We had worked on the Native-American reservations before and we continued that.

> This is democracy in action.

This is democracy in action. I'm proud to say we talked the talk. But we really, *really* walked the walk.

The Mexican-Americans in Texas began to break voting records. Our voting propelled the progressive Lloyd Doggett in the Senate primary race where he edged out a conservative Kent Hance by 509 votes out of nearly 980,000 total votes cast. Who says voting doesn't matter?

At this point, we were turning out to vote at a substantially higher level than the rest of the state (18% of voters compared to 13% of the rest of the state). Way to go, *raza*!

Hasta el taco,
Willie

MAKING MY DREAM COME TRUE, PART 12

GETTING POWER IN THE TIME OF *CHUPACABRAS*

Dear Dreamers:

I let you down in 1984. Reagan won by a landslide. Kicked our butt.... But it wasn't 'cause we didn't register a million people to vote. It was because the Republicans invested serious dollars in massive voter registration throughout the country – and they got the fundamentalist white Christians to vote.

They put $10 million in 28 targeted states. The Democratic Party didn't make anywhere that kind of investment. They relied on us, and we relied on the foundations that were cautious about big funding and early funding....

At this point, SVREP was deemed the "top voter registration organization in the country."

And we were broke. And very tired.

Bien tired,
Willie

Making My Dream Come True, Part 13

BROKE. BUT FOCUS!

Dear Dreamers:

1985. Three years left.

By November of this year, SVREP was facing a deficit of more than $200,000 for the year. The foundations were way too cautious, and the Democratic Party was stumbling. I took out a personal loan against my family's property and secured a $40,000 line of credit for SVREP at a local bank. What else could I do?

My brother George was buying my tacos by then.

I gained weight. I lost weight. I almost lost focus. FOCUS!!!

"We are not here to finish the job, but we are not allowed to stop working either."

This was always burning in my brain. A poet said this. Her name was Elizabeth Bishop.[21]

Tu Willie

---

[21] Elizabeth Bishop, American poet. 1911 – 1979. Considered one of the finest poets of the twentieth century. Willie liked to quote her, but she was paraphrasing from "It is not incumbent upon you to complete the work, but neither are you at liberty to desist from it." (Avot 2:20) or Ethics of the Fathers (Jewish).

MAKING MY DREAM COME TRUE, PART 14

HOW TO KEEP THE *CHUPACABRAS* IN LINE

Dear Dreamers:

The good thing about losing so much is that it helps you focus. Like my mother used to say, *coraje* is a good thing if you use it right...and I wasn't ready to give up.

I knew that it was just as important to believe in our politicians as it was to elect them. If you think they're crooks, you're gonna give up voting. How to make them accountable? I wanted quality, not just quantity.

And then I got into it with Councilman Bernardo Eureste in San Antonio over the Guadalupe Cultural Center....

Train. Focus.

Jump.

So what do you do when the councilman comes to your house to beat you up in the middle of the night? Don't vote for him anymore.

Peace and Love,

Tu Willie

Making My Dream Come True, Part 15

How to Get Power and Not Become a *Chupacabra*

Dear Dreamers,

They say that politics here is more like a telenovela. Well, I became a star in my own soap opera, and looking back at it, I wanna laugh. And cry.

Councilman Bernardo Eureste was a smart, educated, explosive, type of councilman from the barrio. I had been asked to be a board member of the Guadalupe Cultural Center – at the time, they were like the SVREP of the arts: Conjunto; Teatro; Chicano Arts; Book Festival. They were THE S..T. I was super-busy in that summer of 1984, but hey, I love conjunto.

Eureste, also known as "Bennie," had been elected in 1977 as a result of the redistricting. He was also teaching at Our Lady of the Lake University, a Catholic university. He was a love-him-or-hate-him kind of guy. I guess, looking back at it – something like me.

Bennie was really helpful in getting the Guadalupe Cultural Arts Center, the "Guadalupe" off the ground. But then he got *chiflado*. This is what I mean when I say we vote and then we have to keep our politicians responsible. He got spoiled. Arrogant. Threatened to defund the Guadalupe 'cause they were "artistic elitists," and he just didn't like them anymore.

Started calling them names. I'd always supported Bennie, but he was getting crazy 'cause the Guadalupe was going their way, as artists do. On August 23rd, I was so tired. Went home late, then got a weird phone call: "if you go after me I'll have no choice but to go after you." This is really corrupt-talk.

We argued big time. Hung up. Then I got another, weirder, call. From a cantina, probably.

I hung up. Another phone call.

I picked it up. Someone was threatening my family!

Called my brother Ralph who came and picked up my family right away.

He's a former Marine, and he returned to help me rearrange the furniture. Opened the front door so that I could sit on a leather chair and look out to the street. Two hours passed. Then a car drove up, several men in the car. They tried to stare me down. Scary.

This is what I mean about politicians. Sometimes they get crazy with their power. Let them go.

I wrote a letter to the paper saying that WE had to be better than what had come before. We were getting power, alright, but where were we heading?

El Willie

MAKING MY DREAM COME TRUE, PART 16

HOW TO GET POWER AND BECOME BETTER THAN A *CHUPA-CABRA*

Dear Dreamers,

1985. Three years left.

By now, almost 2.7 million Latinos and Latinas were registered to vote in the Southwest. 2,800 elected officials. Our population was growing, and we were getting attention by the mainstream media. We were beginning to have some power. SVREP had begun something, but the voting game was moving ahead with and without us. Good.

It was time for a new set of rules. Now I wanted to focus on what power meant for us. Did we want Reagan-type power or Cesar Chavez-type power?

As Latinos and Latinas, we knew what it was to be powerless. What did we want for ourselves and for everybody who didn't have power, since they included our *abuelitos* and *abuelitas*? Our cousins in prison. Our dropout brother. Our divorced and struggling aunt who'd

been beat up by a *borracho* husband. The kids were starving and going nowhere. What did we really want to become?

Reagan or Cesar Chavez?

I felt like we could set a new music for this country with all that had happened. Or we could be just the same as anyone else.

How to talk about this?

What to do with power once you have it?

Willie

Making My Dream Come True, Part 17

WHAT TO DO WITH POWER: TRAIN AND TRAIN SOME MORE!

Dear Dreamers of the World:

One of the questions I used to get all the time from my Anglo friends all over the country was:

What's wrong with Latinos? Why don't they vote? Why are you guys always dropping out of high school? What's wrong with you? Why don't you read?

I've already explained this in my other letters. Repeat. We mostly come from an agrarian history – working-class, *campesinos*, farmworkers; agrarian is the fancy word. When the Spanish conquistadores came to Mexico, they weren't interested in building a democracy, please. They wanted gold, and the priests, by manipula-ting the natives with their deep belief in gods, were able to have powerful churches.

The Spaniards even married some of us. They repeated what Spain was: A society of classes, and the Spaniards and their descen-dants were at the top. Most of our ancestors were somewhere in the middle or much, much lower. It's been said that in the United States, race is class.

Well, in Mexico and Latin America, it's not about race. It's about class. You get whiter as you move up the ladder...*class is race*.

Got that?

Real voting is non-existent. Education certainly isn't a priority. The situation in the Southwest has not been -- welcoming to the Native Americans and the new mestizos who were our ancestors. You don't build huge ranches like the King Ranch in Texas unless you have lots of cheap labor. There is no slavery except in the mind.... This is called "colonization."

In the United States, voting does count. Not easy, but possible. SVREP proved it.

But how do you explain what Latinos face if they want to vote? What are they thinking? What do they want? What is democracy to them? What kind of Americans are they?

My Jewish friends come from a long tradition of very educated people. We have a long way to go to be at their level this way. That's why I felt we needed more - much more - research.

Train. Back to the beginning. With focus and lots of jumping.

Research in action. Training with lots of focus and jumping.

I called it the Southwest Voter Research Institute.

El Willie

Making My Dream Come True, Part 18

WHAT TO DO WITH POWER: DON'T STOP TRAINING NOW!

Dear Dreamers,

Well, the truth was that SVREP was really broke and I knew the foundations would fund research.

Plus, we really needed money, so why not? We needed to train and share.

In truth,

Willie

MAKING MY DREAM COME TRUE, PART 19

WHAT TO DO WITH POWER/ YOU WILL BE BETRAYED

Dear Dreamers,

1986. Two years left.

We were still broke. The foundations I had counted on were not giving us much money.

Another betrayal. This one almost broke me. This one had to do with a California Senator, Alan Cranston, one of the most powerful Democrats in Congress, who knew he needed Latino votes to win.

He raised lots of money for us from his rich friends. But he didn't give it to us. He kept it for his own campaign.

SVREP had lots of voter registration work to do in California. We badly needed funds. Senator Cranston said that two different organizations that he'd set up would fund us. Basically, they stole my ideas, my experience, my organizing.

I shouldn't have gotten so angry. Should've been more grown-up.

Remember, you will get betrayed in your life! But if you can't move on from it, then they've really beat you up...focus! Focus!

I really took this hard. Wrote hot letters and hotter checks. Got behind, again.

In 1986, it was a banner year for Senator Cranston's re-election effort. But he barely won. Very little of the money he raised went for SVREP. In 1986-87, we completed 96 voter registration drives across 92 cities and 11 American Indian Reservations.

Much later, Senator Cranston was charged with "ethics violations" for other financial activities, and he decided not to seek re-election. I was gone by then...haven't seen him.

Focus.

Willie

Making My Dream Come True, Part 20

WHAT TO DO WITH POWER: FOCUS SO YOU CAN JUMP!

Dear Dreamers around the World,

It was 1987. One year left. One of the best years of my life.

One of my Greek friends from Boston called me. Seems like my old friend, former Governor Michael Dukakis from the Democratic Party, was thinking of running for president. We had met while I was at Harvard a few years back.

My buddy's name was Mitropoulos. He wanted me to be part of the team that Dukakis was setting up. I went. The governor wanted to know:

Who are the "Hispanic" electorate? (The voters).

What do they believe in?

What types of candidates do they support?

What motivates them?

What do they support?

Back in San Antonio, I knew in *mi corazón* how vital Latinos, Hispanics, whatever you want to call us – how important we were to making this country a better place. A democracy. At the same time, our government was deeply involved in revolutions and counter-revolutions in Central America.

I agreed to serve as an advisory board member of the Central American Peace Campaign. We opposed U.S. military intervention in Nicaragua, El Salvador, Guatemala, and other parts of Central America.

You see, I love the democracy part of the U.S. flag. But we are also an empire. I oppose the empire part. If you think Mexico has suffered, then you should see Central America. *Pobrecitos.*

71

In the summer of 1987, I agreed to go on a trip to Chile to help in the democracy-building efforts in that far-away country. Why? Because the U.S. had been involved in a "coup," under President Nixon — which means that our CIA had gotten involved in helping the generals take over the country — despite the fair election of Salvador A-llende.... Lots of activists were brutally killed. Augusto Pinochet took over, and he was a dictator.

Anyway, by 1988, Pinochet felt so much pressure that he held a "referendum," and the mi-litary junta lost! Voting works, you see? Pinochet didn't think the people would vote against him.

So I went as part of a group to help the country prepare for a democracy. Jump. Jump.

Then a month later, I was invited to Honduras, Nicaragua and Costa Rica. Democracy again.

So, the whole time I was doing international diplomacy, what I'd trained for. Now, I was doing it on my terms. Jump.

In democracy,
Willie

MAKING MY DREAM COME TRUE, PART 21

WHAT TO DO WITH POWER: KEEP JUMPING

Dear Dreamers around the world like me:

I'd always believed that U.S. Latinos needed to get involved in international or Latin-American politics. But we had a lot on our plate already. I knew that the people of Latin America wanted democracy, but how can you be good at it if someone doesn't train you first?

How do you teach tolerance for the different? How do we embrace our kind of democracy, which is chaotic and filled with all kinds of religions? How can we help another country begin to see they can create their own kind of democracy without preaching down to them? They will resist it then.

Our democracy is a paradox. You know what that is? A contradiction. The pilgrims didn't arrive in the Americas filled with ideas of democracy. They were escaping religious persecution, and when they got

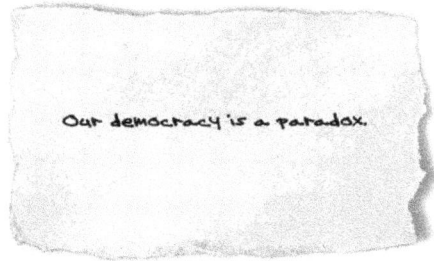

Our democracy is a paradox.

here, it wasn't like they liked the Native Americans worshipping their own gods. Not a good beginning.

We ended up with a Constitution that was created from all kinds of people with democratic practices, including the Native Americans[22]. I don't know if they envisioned what would happen in the new United States, but it did. Slavery and everything.

I call her Lady Destiny. And the whole world wants what we have. We, Latinos, Hispanics, Chicanos, and the women and everyone else, are included in this democracy.

So, I tried to get my community interested in what was happening in Latin America – 'cause it affects us. We were going from the local to the national elections to the international ones. I hoped to see many more in my community travelling to those places I had seen so they could make an impact too – in voting.

In Brown Power,

Willie

_____

[22] "The U.S. Constitution owes its notion of democracy to the Iroquois, including freedom of religion and speech, and separation of powers in government." https://www.politifact.com.

Making My Dream Come True, Part 22

What to Do with Power: Jumping into a New World

Dear Dreamers,

It was 1988. Time to go.

On May 9th of that year, I celebrated turning 44! So old! But I felt 16 and then 76 all at once....

I went off to the East Coast for a conference on the Constitution. Got an award on civil rights. On my way to New York City, I got real, real, tired. Could barely walk.

Returned to San Antonio. The pain. It was so bad that me, Willie Velásquez, superhero, agreed to go to the doctor. Thought it was just bad abdominal pain, like an ulcer.

Was drinking - lots of Pepto Bismal by then, and didn't have health insurance, anyway. Had given it up so there would be more money for SVREP.

It was kidney cancer. Six months to a year to live.

Not afraid...just a little,

Willie

Making My Dream Come True, Part 23

What to do with power: jumping into a new world for real

Dear Dreamers,

Politics to the end.

While I'm at M.D. Anderson in Houston, I find out that Governor Dukakis, who had won the Democratic Party nomination for president, wanted me to be his deputy campaign manager. Nobody really thought I was gonna die – including me. *I'm a hero, and we don't die, right?*

It was great. Lots of people came to visit me at the hospital. Wore me out, too. The cancer was invasive, it was spreading. Sent me home. I got worse.

I was transferred to ICU at the Santa Rosa Hospital in San Antonio.

June 15th, 1988. The Big One wanted me to train and organize the angels, I guess.

I said I'd try. Big One said I needed to examine my life and then... It's been 30 years of examining.

Ok, I'm beginning to examine with these letters?

Que bonito es el otro mundo, right, George?

It's a beautiful world. Jump.

El Willie

Dear Westside Barrio,

You know what I miss the most? The creeks. Weird, right? After all the years of flooding, after the mud that took forever to dry outside and inside our house on Laurel Street. After the mosquitoes eating me alive. And the people who lost their homes. Their lives.

I miss the smell of *frijoles, abuelita's empanadas, carne guisada, caldo de rez,* flour tortillas. Like my mother made, the best of all.

I miss my man-cave on Culebra. It's still there!

Don't worry, it's not like I'm hungry where I am...Not anymore. Just want you to know what it is to miss home.

I miss the low-rider cars and the garages with the tires outside and the hand-lettered signs. *Pintados* all bright. Christmas year-round in San Antonio. I even miss the misspellings, like "loose weight" instead of "lose." Words like "Fideo Thursdays" and "Wátchate." How cool.

I miss the streetlights that don't work. The bumpety streets. The honking after the football games and basketball championships. I can hear those from here, I swear, when you guys win.

I miss the way people talk, like *mande?* At your orders, what a thing to say, where does that come from? Maybe we obey too much.

Mijita, or mijito. My daughter, my son. Which really means my beloved. Because I am older than you and we are all family, really. All of you are my sons. All of you my daughters.

And I really miss hearing – *no te freak*! And *cool arrow,* can I say that? There are other words I miss, but not allowed to use them anymore. The Big One says no. And I obey.

I miss Flaco's accordion. Conjunto just goes with *frijoles,* like the wind blowing through my house on Laurel, the dancing and crying of music on Saturday nights. Why haven't you guys named a school after Flaco and Santiago? What are you waiting for? Don't you realize this music, with all the scales and curly-cues, moaning and whipping up and down and around, is all about us? So much happiness despite everything, in one song? This is our resistance!

I miss the *perros* of the neighborhood, the four-legged ones. Donuts. Pinto. Pinky. Beto. My cats, Fluffy and Smoky and Gato Loco. I remember how Fluffy slept on my chest so I could hardly breathe, while Gato Loco munched on my hair and ear, purring and purring like the accordion late at night, far away in the next block. Take good care of their great-great-great great-grand-million times kitties, please.

I guess I'm homesick. That must be why I'm writing this crazy letter. I miss all of you so much. Do you think of me sometimes? Don't worry, I have everything I need here. But I don't have my barrio....

No regrets.

Dale gas, gente!

FLY.

Willie

Choices

Dear Willie,
Here were your choices:

Life is about the heart.
Life is about things.
Life is, I'm gonna pretend that I don't understand and just float.
Life is about Me.
Life is about Them.
Life is about finding Them in Me and the Me in Them.
I am going to answer my calling no matter what.
I am going to listen to others and please everyone but me.
I am going to get real angry cause I didn't answer my calling
and be mean instead.
I will live my life in fear.
I will never be afraid even when I am.
I will not be afraid to love.
Well done.
You've done real good.
You're home.
San Antonio is waiting for you.

The Big One

Dear papá,

This is the hardest letter of all to write. I don't even remember when you left. Remember the divorce between you and mamá, I was young, married to Janie for a few years.

I will never understand you.

We needed you, the whole family. And you left us. You left us way before the divorce, even.

It was during a time when marriages were not supposed to end like this. When everybody had a father, when we all went to church, when we were innocent.

You know, when I got here, *The New York Times* didn't include you in my obituary. Your name is nowhere; you're barely in my biography by Sepúlveda.

You have grandchildren now. Great-grandchildren. You need to know that your son George and *his* son Alexis are superb photographers...Ralph became a businessman...but you don't care. I heard George's prayers, really, about this book. I'm so proud of everyone. My own children – Carmen, Cata, and Guillermo – incredible people. Thank you, Janie!

And how could I possibly become a good father with you as a role model? Tell me!

I tried in my own way. But I left my children when they needed me. Like you did us. So I tried to save everyone and everything. Spent so much time doing it I didn't save myself.

So, I left my own family without me – after trying to save democracy for this country.

Ha! I found new fathers to replace you: Henry B. González. He also left me 'cause I was a fighter like him but from a different time and place.

Maclovio "Mac" Barraza[23]. He died and left me. How I missed him. I needed a father then.

You were a gambler, papá. A great one, a Las Vegas-type gambler. You could have died there. Well, I gambled too. I risked my life. Lost. But I won, too.

I won for democracy.

I think I found myself now with these letters.

Verdád, San Antonio?

Forevers,

Willie

May 9, 2018
San Antonio, Texas USA

---

[23] A grandson of a copper miner, Barraza rose to become a national union leader of the copper miners. He was a key supporter of voter registration drives in the Southwest, and the founding chairman of the Southwest Voter Registration & Education Project (SVREP). He died in 1980.

The New York Times

Archives | 1988

Willie Velasquez, 44, Hispanic Leader, Dies

Willie Velasquez, a leader of the movement to in-crease political power among Hispanic Americans, died early today of cancer. He was 44 years old.

In 1974 Mr. Velasquez founded the Southwest Voter Registration and Education Project, the nation's larg-est voter registration project aimed at the Hispanic community....

A Note on William "Willie" C. Velásquez

Born May 9, 1944
Died June 15, 1988
(Reborn) May 9, 2018

According to Juan A. Sepúlveda, the author of the first definitive biography of Willie's life[24], Willie directed "one thousand voter registration drives in over two hundred communities across the Southwest and beyond, eighty-five successful voting rights lawsuits and the doubling of the number of Hispanic elected officials from just over 1500 in 1974 to over 3300 in 1988," the year he died.

Most importantly, his Southwest Voter Registration Education Project (SVREP) doubled the number of Latino registered voters to five million by that year as well.

Many consider him to be a hero, a pioneer, a champion of voting rights. But Willie, as he says in his letters here to all of you, was most concerned with democracy.

---

[24] *The Life and Times of Willie Velásquez, Su Voto es Su Voz*, published by Arte Público Press in 2003.

In 1995, Willie received the Presidential Medal of Freedom from President Bill Clinton in ceremonies at the White House. His widow, Janie, received the medal in his place.

Willie had more he wanted to do before he left us. He wanted to educate us more than helping us fill out a voting registration card. He wanted to help us understand the political machinery of voting, how to participate in a democracy so that it listened to us, how to make our elected officials responsible, how to share our democracy with the rest of the world.

He was convinced that Latinos could and would make a contribution. I think he was right, and that's why AALAS selected his story for the first book in our (S)Hero's Journey Series.

His speeches were many, smart, and verbose. Consider these his private letters; you are hearing his personal, kitchen-table voice. He wanted young people especially, to understand his life.

Because Willie was such a good student, he used the Spanish rules of names, and so the accents here are grammatically correct – even if they are not our "Tejano" way, because he wants the Mexicans to read this book too.

Most of all, don't forget who he was. He never forgot you.

For more information on Willie, check out our Select Sources page. See you at the voting booth!

Bárbara Renaud González

ACKNOWLEDGEMENTS

When Willie Velásquez left us, over 2000 people attended his funeral. Presidential candidate Michael Dukakis attended. The Brown Berets saluted him. The community came out to honor him, lining the streets from the Westside to San Fernando Cemetery, where he is buried.

I was living in Dallas, Texas, at the time, and wanted to come to the funeral. "Why, did you know him?" my husband asked. I had never met him but knew some of what he meant to all of us. This is my way of attending his funeral.

I want to thank George and Andrea Velásquez for lending me the money to begin the children's book that Willie deserved. And his late mother, Mary Louise Velásquez, who so graciously shared the few photos she had left and told me good stories about Willie as a child.

Gracias to all of Willie's siblings: George; Stella; Ralph; David, and his children: Carmen, "Cata," and Guillermo, who have always been patient with my questions. I don't think I will ever understand what it is to lose your father so early. With this book, I want you to know that I am trying to listen to his best self.

I really want to thank St. Mary's University, Dr. Jerry Poyo, but especially Dr. Charles Cotrell, President Emeritus, and Willie's mentor, for his guidance through the many obstacles in getting this book completed – and for taking the time to guide me through Willie's political life in a way that I could translate to the average person. I will never be the same again.

To Janie Velásquez: one day your story will be told. Thank you for loving Willie forever.

And a special thanks to the AALAS board of directors for your belief in my dreams for this book: Gloria de Leon; Denise McVea; Terri Flores Lopez; Nadine Saliba. And to Mary Lou Gomez-Rittie for giving me so much permission when I said this was a calculated risk.

Many people donated to the small and very big costs in creating a book like this. It takes a barrio like Willie says. A pueblo, a country of commitment. I want to especially thank Domingo Garcia, attorney-at-law, for welcoming me into the world of voter registration over 25 years ago in Dallas. It began there and continued with your critical financial support.

Thank you especially to the Dudley T. Dougherty Foundation and the estate of Mariana S. Ornelas. This book is shining proof of your generosity and love.

With your support, you provided the impetus that allowed me to study the life of Willie Velásquez and to imagine this book as a touchstone for years to come.

Willie Velásquez has been in my dreams for so long. Every single one of you should be proud that you helped Willie find his way back home. A book like this is his gift to all of you. Now, he is home with us.

Ahora, to tell the other stories of so many (S)Heroes of our beloved Texas. But there is no one like El Willie.

Adelante con this book, *con* voting, and remember that you have a voice!

Bárbara Renaud González
San Antonio, Texas
May 9, 2018

Select Sources

Velásquez, William C., by Cynthia E . Orozco
The Handbook of Texas Online
tshaonline.org

Willie Velásquez 1944-1988, *The Texas Observer*, July 29, 1988

Willie Velásquez, 44, Hispanic Leader, Dies
The New York Times, June 16, 1988

Willie Velásquez; Leader of Latino Political Movement
Los Angeles Times, June 16, 1988

Children's Biography of Willie Velásquez gets preview today
San Antonio Express-News, May 8, 2012

Recognition day set for Willie Velásquez
San Antonio Express-News, April 7, 2014

Film:

Hillcrest celebrates Willie Velásquez Day, May 9, 2014, Youtube.com
(two videos)

PBS Special: Your Vote is Your Voice, September 2016
Directed by Hector Galán

Willie Velásquez and Early Attempts to Reach Latino Voters,
Time.com, October 3, 2016

ABOUT AALAS

A lazán Arts Letters & Stories is a 501(c)3 non-profit organization founded in 2015 to tell the stories of the marginalized (s)heroes of Texas.

Our website is www.alazanstories.org.

Forthcoming books in the (S)Heroes Journey include the following biographies:

Rosie Castro: How to Raise Boys to be Good Men

Gus Garcia: Supreme Lawyer Meets the Supreme Court

Lydia Mendoza: I always wanted a guitar

Américo Paredes: TBD

Jovita Idar: TBD

Manuela Solís de Sager: The Hell-Raiser in the Pecans

Raul Salinas: Pinto, Poet, Philosopher

Lucy González Parsons: A Love Story under the Texas Moon

Angela de Hoyos: TBD

Gloria Anzaldúa: TBD

AALAS is our literary way of spelling wings in Spanish, *alas*. Alazán is the name of a creek in San Antonio that runs through the barrio. In Spanish, it means "chestnut," or "sorrel" for the chestnut horses that the Mexicans and Spaniards rode through here. Alazán is Andalusían Arabic (reddish-brown, sorrel).

About the Author

B árbara Renaud González is a writer born in Texas. Her father was born on the King Ranch, and her mother was from Mexico. Her father was a sharecropper and her mother worked as a nurse's aide. Her family loves books; almost all her brothers and sisters have finished college. As the oldest of eight, she saw how her parents always, always, voted, even when they had to pay a poll tax.

In 1967, the Chicano Movement and the tumult of the Civil Rights Movement changed her life. Because of all the protests and marches that were happening around her, she was able to attend and graduate from the University of Michigan at Ann Arbor – for free – with a Master's degree in Social Work. She worked very hard in all that snow and got the chance to work in Washington D.C. and met Senator Ted Kennedy. Later, she was able to attend the Harvard Kennedy School of Public Affairs and learned more about labor rights and immigration.

Through all of this, she always read all the books she could and wrote secretly. Like Willie, she finally listened to her calling, and has now written four books and is working on a fairy tale for adults. It is about a girl who is the daughter of the moon....

Bárbara thinks of herself as an artist who believes in the power of democracy to make the world a better place. She says that she dreams of Willie and that she is learning to listen better to the universe.

She hopes that you like her book and hopes that you will listen to your own calling, like Willie did.

INDEX